Coming Home

POEMS ON THE WAY HOME

Saskia Scott

Copyright © 2024 by Saskia Scott

All rights reserved. No part of this book may be reproduced in any manner whatsoever without written permission except in the case of brief quotations embodied in critical articles and reviews.

First Printing, 2024

Cover image by S. Hermann and F. Richter via Pixabay @ pixel2013

Written and edited by Saskia Scott

With thanks to the unending support of my husband Beren Scott, Pam and Barry Kubank, Ana Guthridge, Helen Hewitt, and so many more.

Contents

Dedication   v

One
The Orphan   1

The Orphan   5

The Orphan   12

Two
Poems   14

Threads   15

Now   16

Sunrise   17

Hot Air Balloons   18

Change   19

Balance   20

Wave   22

Woman Become Brave   23

Integrity   24

Anxiety   25

Two Loves	26
Racham	27
Return	28
Raindrops	29
The Seed	30
Anhinga, Anhinga	31
The Light in the Well	32
Dawn at Darkan	34
Coming Home	35

One

The Orphan

A Fairytale

The Orphan

Once upon a time there was a little girl whose parents died. She was lonely but she was so scared that she stayed in the house until all the firewood had run out, and all the food and water too, so that she was cold and hungry and thirsty, and then she stayed long past that.

When she couldn't bear it any longer, she wandered out into the woods. She met a mother bear who helped her find food and let her ride on her back when she was tired. When the girl was lonely and cold and sad the bear would curl up next to her in her cozy den. When the girl was frightened, the mother bear would chase all the bad things away.

The Orphan

One day the girl got on the bear's back and the bear took her to a big house where lots of orphans lived. They all played together and the girl slowly grew up. Then one day, when the girl had become a young woman, the bear took her to a high cliff overlooking a vast blue sea. The sunlight sparkled on the waves.

A flock of terns were sitting on the edge of the cliff and when the woman arrived they all flew away. The woman longed to go with them on their adventure, but she had no wings. She ran back to the bear, but the bear only nudged her back towards the cliff again. The woman noticed there was one last tern waiting. He was waiting for her. The bear gently bit the woman's arm, and growled softly. The woman knew what it meant, but she was frightened. She watched as the last tern took off and soared into the wide blue sky. It turned its head to look back at her.

'Follow me,' its eyes seemed to say.

The Orphan

The woman took a breath and ran towards the edge of the cliff. She knew the bear would be waiting for her whenever she needed her. But now it was time to go on a journey.

As she leapt over the edge, instead of plummeting to the ground as she feared, she felt wings sprout from her back. She flapped them to rise higher into the sky and looked ahead at the tern leading the way. She wasn't sure where she was going, but she was free now, and an orphan no more. She knew that the bird was leading her to home, joy and peace. She could trust him, and she could feel her own wings growing stronger the further she flew.

The tern led her over a dark patch of ocean. The darkness was like a mirror where she could see dirt and mud that was caked on her wings. The mud made it harder to fly. Shaking it off was hard. The tern had to lead her to a whirlpool to get rid of some of it. It was scary in the black whirlpool, but the tern was still there and the woman trusted him.

The Orphan

The woman and the tern came back out of the whirlpool and flew high above the vast, wide blue sea. White caps came and went as they looked down and in the distance were some islands. They were flying there together. The woman flapped her wings. They were strong and broad. A lot could fall under the shadow of her wings.

'What were you doing all my life?' she asked the tern. 'Where were you when I was lonely and hungry and cold?'

The tern circled around her, dipping and darting and diving playfully.

'Think back,' he said.

The woman thought. She remembered back to the cold, dark house with its grimy windows. Out of one window she remembered she could see a patch of sky. And yes, she remembered sometimes there had been a winged shape, dipping and darting and wheeling against the blue. And, from time to time, a feather on the sill.

The Orphan

She heard the tern speak.

"You didn't know I was there then, but I helped you. I gave you clues about how to survive until you had the strength to leave that house and find the mother bear. And when you were strong enough, but still hesitating, I came down one night and gave you an extra fan with my wings to help you along.'

They kept soaring in silence. The woman cried as she flew and her tears fell down, down, down into the ocean where they added their salt to the salt of the waves. She'd thought she had no one. She'd thought no one was there to help her, that she could rely on no one, that she was entirely by herself. But she had been wrong. The tern had been watching over her all that time. The tern looked back at her with his jewel-like eyes. He spoke again.

"I am very proud of you," he said.

The Orphan

The woman could see an island up ahead. The tern was taking her there. As they got closer, she saw a house. It looked familiar and she felt her stomach tighten. It was her old house.

"I thought I'd left it behind," she said as they landed.

"You did," said Mama Bear, who was there to greet them. "But you left some important parts of yourself there too. It's time to get them back."

The tern gave the woman a crown made of red wood and rose gold. There were places for jewels in it, but they were empty. The woman walked through the rooms of the house and as she did she remembered. She realised she had left some of her soul with each bad memory, so that she could forget.

"You're strong enough now," said the tern.

"Yes," said the bear. "They will make your crown more beautiful."

The Orphan

So over many days the woman found the jewels that had the pieces of her soul one by one. She washed them with her tears and looked at them from every angle to see how the light shone through them. Then she put each one in its place in her crown. But the centre jewel was still missing.

"That is for another time," said the tern.

They flew on. As they flew, the woman started to look around. She wondered how her heavy body could be carried by her wings. Suddenly she became very afraid of the long drop to the deep dark ocean below. She started falling.

"Help!" she cried out.

The Orphan

The tern came and lifted her with his beak as though she was feather light.

"You are not heavy," he said, "but the memory of the house is, and the fear of it heavier still."

"I thought when I found the jewels in my crown, that I would be healed."

"Fear will always come back at times, but you can defeat it by choosing to live with love and freedom. It is time to rest again, and I will show you."

The tern took her to another island. This one had a small cabin, and Mama Bear was waiting there again. In front of the cabin was a large labyrinth.

"Journey into the centre," said the tern.

The Orphan

The woman walked the labyrinth, and she understood. She could journey to her own centre, her own essence, and there she was safe from fear. There she would find the final missing jewel from her crown. All she needed was to be willing to make the journey.

"Let us rest here a while first," the tern said. "There is one more person for you to meet before we go on."

The woman went inside and fell asleep wrapped up in the warmth of Mama Bear's paws, just as she had used to.
The woman, the bear and the tern stayed at the island for a long time. Each morning the woman would sit by the sea and each evening she walked the labyrinth. The bear and the tern taught her where to find food and she was content to enjoy the beautiful island and keep her cabin clean and tidy. One morning, she was sweeping, and looking out the window to the sea. She looked down to her broom, and there sitting by her feet was the most beautiful jewel she had ever seen, shining golden in the morning light.

The Orphan

She took off her crown and tried it – it fit perfectly. She looked back to the window, and there was the tern with a fish in his beak.

"Breakfast?" he said, his eyes sparkling.

"I thought I had to make a long journey to find this!" the woman stammered.

"You are always making it."

This was a new voice, melodic and rich. The woman turned and in the doorway stood the most gloriously beautiful lady she had ever seen. She was richly dressed in gold and purple silk, and her thick shining hair was crowned with a garland. Her ample curves made the woman think of generous abundance and verdant fields.

"I am Wisdom," said the lady. "If you ever need me, all you need to do is ask, and I will come to you."

The Orphan

She gently took the crown out of the woman's hands, and put it back on her head.

"Beautiful," she said, smiling.

Together, the woman, Lady Wisdom, the bear and the tern had breakfast. Then the tern said,

"It is time to go," and they flew again.

"But where are we going?" asked the woman.

"We are following the light."

Two

Poems

Threads

Green growth stitches my heart,
a leafy thread of vine pulling
the cracked pieces together.
I follow the thread.
Its tendrils weave
through the corners of my past,
the pages of history,
the hearts of those who seek healing
from the aloe of its sap
till it returns, at last, to where it began;
the rugged tree of life
standing in the garden at dawn,
and I see, it is very good.

Now

This moment is yours
but not for holding.
You cannot lose it.

No need to grasp.
Only to be.

Sunrise

It's early, and last night's cold
has not quite leeched
from my frozen feet.

I walk in warm shallows.
Slow dawn air carries a stink
of seaweed and kerosene.

The dead husk of a tiny crab,
one claw gone,
dances in the pull of wavelets

with detritus
and the bell-shaped bodies
of translucent stingers.

An osprey spirals slowly,
still-winged,
in search of fish.

The sea writhes with life and death
as the sand-scrubbed day takes breath.

Hot Air Balloons

In early hours
we moved torpidly along arterial roads.
The months that had been
were still ringing in my heart,
clouding my head with confusion and
peripheral sorrow.

Banked up traffic allowed me
small islands of peace.
Then, like a dream, suddenly, I saw
first one, then three, six,
ten hot air balloons,
their bright fires flaring erratically.
Like colourful jewels
floating impossibly
against the pink dawn sky.
An oasis amid chaos,
their image still warms me,
fills me,
buoys me up.

Change

My old life lies at my feet
in a jumble of socks
and shirts and underwear.
Change has stretched me out of shape
for them, but I linger
as if I could fit myself back in.

Like the skin of some insect
it clings to me;
the final step away
into the new
must shake it off,
no matter how roughly. A step
that will thrust me out of myself
if I dare.

Balance

Imagine a balance
or a see-saw
with a boulder resting on one side.
You are pushing down on the other
to even out the beam,
pushing with your whole self, muscles
shaking.

Or imagine you are trying to pull free a rope
or length of fabric trapped
in the earth under a mountainous rock,
leaning back, digging in your heels,
straining.

Imagine
you have been doing this for months
years
longer than you can remember.
So long you don't remember
or pay mind to the effort.

Then the fabric snaps.
The boulder disappears.
The weight of the world changes.
You lose your footing,
hit the earth with a thud
of bruising flesh
as you try to make sense
of a dense absence.

That is what it was like
when my mother died
and I realised all my striving had been anchored to her.

Now the heavy threat of her is replaced
by a disorienting weightlessness
and I am left sitting
exhausted
as the trembling leaves my bones.

No need to keep pushing and pulling
as though the rock is still there.
Rest now.
Rebalance.

Wave

I swirl all around it.
Every angle
proves unyielding.
When will I stop returning
to this obstinate truth?

Will I ever, like water,
wear it down
to a pebble I can toss away?

Or will the weight of your absent love
remain within me,
stone like?

Woman Become Brave

Flex my hands in the
earth and
knead the fertile, rising dough.

Hear the song of the birds;
the deep calling to deep.

If I must step back, push forward
again, fists to the wall
bearing down
sweat, blood + birth.

I will run my race.
I will walk on my own feet.
I will whisper my truth into the wild wind
and find my north star
bursting from within my own darkness.

Integrity

My heart lay open,
your pain leaked in,
became mine
and you looked at me
like a mirror.

Stitch me up
hem me in
make me safe behind the walls
of who I am.

Who I am.

I am free,
myself.
I am
not you.

Anxiety

Wind.
Slow-rolling, white threaded waves
with their veneer of rain
heaving up to meet the grey horizon.

Tightness,
squeezing my chest, my throat,
am I enough?
What if? What if? If only...

I sit and watch the fickle sea;
its surface seems
as troubled as my mind.

But the sea doesn't care for self-attack,
and beneath its restless breakers lies a deep
and subtle stillness.

My breath rolls into my lungs.
I pull it from the clouded sky,
breath it back into the world warm
and slow.

I watch my tossing thoughts,
plunge beneath them,
find the silent depths teeming with life.

Two Loves

1.
A warm smile in my chest when you are here.
Obsession, a squeezing pain when you are not.
We talk
Share the same struggles, the same fears,
the same power, the same flaws.
You seem to know me
And there is something about you
that I recognise.
I love you
Because I love myself.

2.
An ambivalent love
Confusion, struggle, wrestling to express
My Self with you.
Sensuous and erotic,
My body tingles as I feel you move.
Afraid to come too close or stray too far.
We grow together,
A partnership,
Making something new.
I love you
Because you are your Self.

Racham

For a miscarried child

dirt stains sidewalk
like mulberry
black blood clots -

my heart's blood

spilled for you
my small one
who I never saw...

Return

As we sail over air currents
patches of salt-parched earth,
quilted together like
rusted metal and plywood,
fade doggedly into the peculiar green
of Australian bush.

We alight into
a warm evening breeze
carrying sharp scents of salt
and wildfire;
the smell of home.

Raindrops

she gave birth
to the three of us
with a cursing thunder

my mother;
a dark, towering cloud
threw us down

through brewing electric dark;
hurled us
toward the unforgiving earth.

she obliterates our sky and yet
where we fall, seeds grow
and something of her is in them.

The Seed

Gropes and writhes through
twists and turns
past bits of broken rock
and earthworms.

A tiny tendril,
fat with milk of rich seed,
peeks out,
leaf upturned, a tender green

palm catching a cascade of light.
So it grows, roots twined around my heart,
a fresh new hope
out of the secret dark.

Anhinga, Anhinga

Beautiful bird,
your sharp-eyed head atop a sinuous neck,
your tail a gown
drifting beneath dappled brown
water.

You submerge
and re-emerge triumphant,
a silvered fish
speared upon your beak.

Anhinga, anhinga,
teach me how
you search beneath the surface.
I want to learn the art
of breaking through the murk
clutching a glittering gift.

The Light in the Well

I found a child hiding in a garden.
She was huddled with her arms around her knees.
I stooped to look at her. I held out my hand.
She took it.

I led her away from there, from the garden,
through the gate in the wall,
out to a wide field
where a deep well was.

We sat by it together,
the child and I.
"Look," I said, and pointed.

There were fish in the well
and wind rippled the face of the water.
"Look deeper."

Beneath it all,
the child saw at last,
a jewel-like light inhabited the depths.

"What is it?" she asked.

"It is your light and my light
The light at the heart of us all.
It can never be extinguished,
not even when wind and storm churn the water."

We go back often, the child and I,
to gaze at the glimmering light.
And there we find our peace.

Dawn at Darkan

Dawn reaches
pale golden fingertips
past frozen sleeping fields.

Beauty refracts through diamonds
at the end
of a dark, cold night.

Coming Home

After a long winter
lost among shifting ice floes
there comes a day,
suddenly,
when the first spring flower emerges
and the sun's rays feel warm
again.

And arising from behind the mists,
inexplicably there,
as mysteriously as it disappeared,
the familiar shape of the place I once called home.

I knew every corridor, every nook,
& every loose floorboard.
How could I forget this place?
How could I forget the way there?

Yet here it is
once more, as I left it.
Every book in its right place.
The parts of me I thought I left behind;
that I hid for safekeeping,
like a buried treasure in a stony field.

Thank you for reading

If these poems brought up anything for you, I recommend you look at the following resources:

- If you are in crisis call Lifeline on 13 11 14 or 000
- To talk to someone about childhood trauma call Blue Knot Foundation on 1300 657 380 or go to blueknot.org.au
- For peer support recovery from childhood trauma go to adultchildren.com.au

For more of my work

Find me on Instagram @sasswritespoems
Or at my website saskiamarinascott.wixsite.com/sasswrites

www.ingramcontent.com/pod-product-compliance
Lightning Source LLC
Chambersburg PA
CBHW062044290426
44109CB00026B/2722